D0292995

In Honor of the Graduate

_____

Presented By

_____

BB

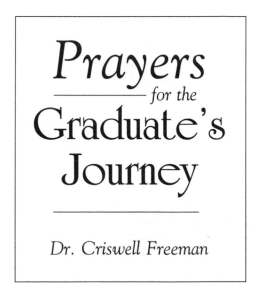

Prayers
for the
Graduate's
Journey

Dr. Criswell Freeman

Brighton Books
Nashville, TN

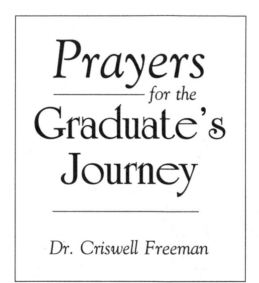

Prayers
for the
Graduate's
Journey

Dr. Criswell Freeman

BRIGHTON BOOKS
Nashville, TN 37204

ISBN 1-58334-130-7

The quoted ideas expressed in this book (but not scripture verses) are not, in all cases, exact quotations, as some have been edited for clarity and brevity. In all cases, the author has attempted to maintain the speaker's original intent. In some cases, quoted material for this book was obtained from secondary sources, primarily print media. While every effort was made to ensure the accuracy of these sources, the accuracy cannot be guaranteed. For additions, deletions, corrections or clarifications in future editions of this text, please write BRIGHTON BOOKS.

All scripture quotations, unless otherwise indicated, are taken from the HOLY BIBLE, NEW INTERNATIONAL VERSION ©. NIV ©. Copyright © 1973, 1978, 1984, by International Bible Society. Used by permission of Zondervan Publishing House. All rights reserved.

Scripture taken from *THE MESSAGE*. Copyright © 1993, 1994,1995,1996. Used by permission of NavPress Publishing Group.

Scripture taken from the NEW AMERICAN STANDARD BIBLE®, Copyright © 1960, 1962, 1963, 1968, 1971, 1972, 1973, 1975, 1977, 1995 by The Lockman Foundation. Used by permission.

Scripture quotations marked (NLT) are taken from The Holy Bible, New Living Translation, Copyright © 1996. Used by permission of Tyndale House Publishers, Incorporated, Wheaton, Illinois 60189. All rights reserved.

Printed in the United States of America
Cover Design & Page Layout: *Bart Dawson*

1 2 3 4 5 6 7 8 9 10 • 02 03 04 05 06 07 08 09 10

Acknowledgments: The author is indebted to Angela Freeman for her support and friendship. The help of the wonderful staff at Walnut Grove Press has made the writing of this book pleasurable and much easier.

Dedication to you,
the Graduate

Table of Conents

A Prayer for the Journey...

How to Use This Book

Because you are reading a book with the word *graduate's* in its title, it's likely that congratulations are in order. If you have recently graduated—or are about to—please accept a metaphorical pat on the back. You've earned it.

Now that your graduation is past, you may be facing a multitude of decisions: where to live, where to work, what to do about your personal relationships. These decisions are important, of course, but they pale in comparison to a single overriding choice that will fashion your eternal destiny. That decision is your commitment to form a personal, saving relationship with Jesus Christ.

Daily life is woven together with the threads of habit, and no habit is more important to your spiritual growth than the discipline of daily prayer and devotion to God. This little book is intended to help. This text is divided into 31 chapters, one for each day of the month. During the next 31 days, please try this experiment: Read a chapter each day. If you're already committed to a daily worship time, this book will enrich that experience. If you are not, the simple act of giving God a few minutes each morning will change the tone and direction of your life.

You have worked hard to graduate, and you are about to embark upon the journey of a lifetime.

If you make every step of that journey with Christ by your side—and if you build your faith upon the firm foundation of God's promises—you will claim for yourself the abundance and grace that God intends for your life. So today, if you do nothing else, accept God's grace with open arms. When you do, you will be the proud recipient of a priceless graduation gift that will change your life forever and endure throughout eternity.

Yet, O LORD, you are our Father.
We are the clay, you are the potter;
we are all the work of your hand.

—

Isaiah 64:8 NIV

A Prayer for
the Journey...
With Christ

Jesus said to them,
"I am the bread of life; he who
comes to Me will not hunger,
and he who believes in Me
will never thirst."

John 6:35 NASB

There's an old saying—trite but true—"Today is the first day of the rest of your life." As a recent graduate, you are beginning a new life. Perhaps it's time to move on to the halls of higher learning, or perhaps you're venturing into the workplace. Whatever your situation may be, remember that this day holds boundless possibilities *if* you are wise enough and observant enough to claim them.

For Christian believers, every day begins and ends with God and His Son. Christ came to this earth to give us abundant life and eternal salvation. Our task is to accept Christ's grace with joy in our hearts and praise on our lips.

Believers who fashion their days around Jesus are transformed: They see the world differently, they act differently, and they feel differently about themselves and their neighbors. Christian believers face the inevitable challenges and disappointments of each day armed with the joy of Christ and the promise of salvation. So whatever this day holds for you, begin it and end it with God as your partner and Christ as your Savior. And throughout the day, give thanks to the One who created you and saved you. God's love for you is infinite. Accept it joyously and be thankful.

Take my yoke upon you, and learn of me;
for I am meek and lowly in heart: and ye shall
find rest unto your souls. For my yoke is easy,
and my burden is light.

Jesus
Matthew 11:29-30 KJV

True have his promises been; not one has failed.
I want none beside him. In life he is my life,
and in death he shall be the death of death;
in poverty, Christ is my riches; in sickness,
he makes my bed; in darkness, he is my star,
and in brightness, he is my sun; he is the manna
of the camp in the wilderness, and he shall be
the new corn of the host when they come to
Canaan. Jesus is to me all grace and no wrath,
all truth and no falsehood; and of truth and
grace he is full, infinitely full.

C. H. Spurgeon

The secret is Christ in me, not me
in a different set of circumstances.

Elisabeth Elliot

Has he taken over your heart?
Perhaps he resides there,
but does he preside there?

Vance Havner

Today's Prayer

Dear Jesus, I know that you
are the bread of life and the Savior
of my life. When I am weak,
You give me strength, and when I am
worried, You give me peace. Thank you,
Lord, for the gift of eternal life and for
the gift of eternal love. May I be ever
grateful, and may I share Your good
news with a world that so desperately
needs Your healing grace.

Amen

A Prayer for
the Journey...
Faith

And Jesus answered and said to
them, "Truly I say to you, if you
have faith and do not doubt…
even if you say to this mountain,
'Be taken up and cast into the sea,'
it will happen."

Matthew 21:21 NASB

In the months and years ahead, your faith will be tested many times. Every life—including yours—is a series of successes and failures, celebrations and disappointments, joys and sorrows. Every step of the way, through every triumph and tragedy, God will stand by your side and strengthen you…*if* you have faith in Him.

Jesus taught his disciples that if they had faith, they could move mountains. You can too. If you place your faith, your trust, indeed your life in the hands of Christ Jesus, you'll be amazed at the marvelous things He can do with you and through you.

Faith is a willingness to believe in things that are unseeable and to trust in things that are unknowable. Today and every day, strengthen your faith through praise, through worship, through Bible study, and through prayer. God has big plans for you, so trust His plans and strengthen your faith in Him. With God, all things are possible, and He stands ready to help you accomplish miraculous things with your life…*if* you have faith.

Now Faith...is the art of holding on to things
your reason has once accepted, in spite of your
changing moods. For moods will change....
That is why Faith is such a necessary virtue:
unless you teach your moods "where they get off,"
you can never be either a sound Christian
or even a sound atheist, but just a creature
dithering to and fro, with its beliefs really
dependent on the weather and the state
of its digestion. Consequently one must
train the habit of Faith.

C. S. Lewis

Faith means believing in realities that go
beyond sense and sight...being aware
of unseen divine realities all around you.

Joni Eareckson Tada

Faith never knows where it is being led,
but it loves the One who is leading.

Oswald Chamrbers

For in the gospel a righteousness is being
revealed, a righteousness that is by faith
from first to last, just as it is written:
"The righteous will live by faith."

Romans 1:17 NIV

Today's Prayer

Dear God, sometimes this world can be a fearful place, full of uncertainty and doubt. In those dark moments, help me to remember that You are always near and that You can overcome any challenge. Give me faith and let me remember always that with Your love and Your power, I can live courageously and faithfully today and every day.

Amen

A Prayer for
the Journey...
Celebration

This is the day which the Lord
hath made; we will rejoice
and be glad in it.

Psalm 118:24 KJV

The 118th Psalm reminds us that today, like every other day, is a cause for celebration. God gives us this day, He fills it to the brim with possibilities, and He challenges us to use it for His purposes. The day is presented to us fresh and clean at midnight, free of charge, but we must beware: Today is a non-renewable resource—once it's gone, it's gone forever. Our responsibility, of course, is to use this day in the service of God's will and according to His commandments.

Today, treasure the time that God has given you. Give Him the glory and the praise and the thanksgiving that He deserves. And search for the hidden possibilities that God has placed along your path. This day is a priceless gift from God, so use it joyfully and encourage others to do likewise. After all, this is the day the Lord has made….

Rejoicing is clearly a spiritual command.
To ignore it, I need to remind you,
is disobedience.

Chuck Swindoll

There is not one blade of grass, there is no color
in this world that is not intended
to make us rejoice.

John Calvin

Christ is not only a remedy for your weariness
and trouble, but he will give you an abundance
of the contrary, joy and delight. They who come
to Christ, do not only come to a resting-place
after they have been wandering in a wilderness,
but they come to a banqueting-house where they
may rest, and where they may feast. They may
cease from their former troubles and toils,
and they may enter upon a course of delights
and spiritual joys.

Jonathan Edwards

So now we can rejoice in our wonderful new
relationship with God—all because of what our
Lord Jesus Christ has done for us in making us
friends of God.

Romans 5:11 NLT

Today's Prayer

Lord God, You have created a grand
and glorious universe that is far beyond
human understanding. The heavens
proclaim Your handiwork, and every star
in the sky tells of Your power. Let me
celebrate You and Your marvelous
creation, Lord, and let me rejoice in this
day and every day, now and forever.
Today is Your gift to me, Lord. Let me
use it to Your glory while giving all
the praise to You.

Amen

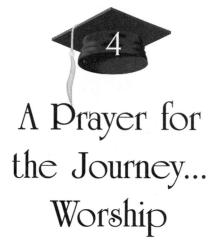

A Prayer for
the Journey...
Worship

Then saith Jesus unto him, Get thee
hence, Satan: for it is written, Thou
shalt worship the Lord thy God, and
him only shalt thou serve.

Matthew 4:10 KJV

All of mankind is engaged in the practice of worship. Some choose to worship God and, as a result, reap the joy that He intends for His children. Others distance themselves from God by worshiping such things as earthly possessions or personal gratification…and when they do so, they suffer.

When we place our desires for material possessions above our love for God—or when we yield to temptations of the flesh—we find ourselves engaged in a struggle that is similar to the one Jesus faced when He was tempted by Satan. In the wilderness, Satan offered Jesus earthly power and unimaginable riches, but Jesus turned Satan away and chose instead to worship only God. We must do likewise by putting God first and by worshiping only Him.

When we worship God, either alone or in the company of fellow believers, we are blessed. When we fail to worship God, for whatever reason, we forfeit the spiritual riches that are rightfully ours. Every day provides opportunities to put God where He belongs: at the center of our lives. Let us worship Him and only Him today and always.

The New Testament does not envisage solitary religion; some kind of regular assembly for worship and instruction is everywhere taken for granted in the Epistles.

C. S. Lewis

I was glad when they said unto me, Let us go into the house of the LORD.

Psalm 122:1 KJV

Worship the Lord with gladness. Come before him, singing with joy. Acknowledge that the Lord is God! He made us, and we are his. We are his people, the sheep of his pasture.

Psalm 100:2-3 NLT

In the sanctuary, we discover beauty: the beauty of His presence.

Kay Arthur

Today's Prayer

Lord, this world is a place of distractions and temptations. But when I worship You, Lord, you set my path—and my heart— straight. Let this day and every day be a time of worship. Whether I am in Your house of worship or simply going about my daily activities, let me worship You not only with words and deeds but also with my heart. In the quiet moments of the day, let me praise You and thank You for creating me, loving me, guiding me, and saving me.

Amen

A Prayer for the Journey... Sharing the Good News

> For God has not given us a spirit of timidity, but of power and love and discipline. Therefore do not be ashamed of the testimony of our Lord....
>
> *2 Timothy 1: 7-8 NASB*

In his second letter to Timothy, Paul shares a message to believers of every generation when he writes, "God has not given us a spirit of timidity." Paul's meaning is crystal clear: When sharing our testimonies, we, as Christians, must be courageous, forthright, and unashamed.

We live in a world that desperately needs the healing message of Christ Jesus. Every believer, each in his or her own way, bears responsibility for sharing the Good News of our Savior. It is important to remember that we bear testimony through both words and actions. Wise Christians follow the admonition of St. Francis of Assisi who advised, "Preach the gospel at all times and, if necessary, use words."

If you are a believer in Christ, you know how He has touched your heart and changed your life. Now is the time to share your testimony with others. So today, preach the Gospel through your words *and* your deeds...but not necessarily in that order.

Go. This is the command of our Lord. Where?
To the world, for it is the world that is on God's
heart. Out there are multitudes for whom Christ
died. And the minute you and I receive the
light of the gospel we, at that moment, become
responsible for spreading that light to those
who are still in darkness.

Kay Arthur

In their heart of hearts, I think all true followers
of Christ long to become contagious Christians.
Though unsure about how to do so or the risks
involved, deep down they sense that there isn't
anything as rewarding as opening a person up
to God's love and truth.

Bill Hybels

Jesus made Himself known to His own,
and if others are to hear about him today,
you and I must tell them.

Vance Havner

But ye shall receive power, after that the
Holy Ghost is come upon you: and ye shall be
witnesses unto me both in Jerusalem, and
in all Judea, and in Samaria, and unto the
uttermost part of the earth.

Acts 1:8 KJV

Today's Prayer

Dear Lord, You sent Your Son Jesus
to die on a cross for me. Jesus
endured indignity, suffering, and death
so that I might live. Because He lives,
I, too, have Your promise of eternal life.
Let me share this good news, Lord, with
a world that so desperately needs Your
healing hand and the salvation of Your
Son. Today, let me share the message of
Jesus Christ through words and deeds.

Amen

A Prayer for the Journey... Living a Righteous Life

Blessed are those who hunger
and thirst for righteousness,
for they will be filled.

Matthew 5:6 NIV

God has given us a guidebook for righteous living called the Holy Bible. It contains thorough instructions which, if followed, lead to fulfillment, righteousness and salvation. But, if we choose to ignore God's commandments, the results are as predictable as they are tragic.

A righteous life has many components: faith, honesty, generosity, love, kindness, humility, gratitude, and worship, to name but a few. If we seek to follow the steps of our Savior, Jesus Christ, we must seek to live according to His commandments. In short, we must, to the best of our abilities, live according to the principles contained in God's Holy Word.

As a recent graduate, you are embarking upon a new phase of life. Wherever you travel, God is there, so make Him your traveling companion. Study God's Word and live by it. Make your life a shining example for those who have not yet found Christ. Embrace righteousness.

And, for further instructions, read the manual.

There may be no trumpet sound or loud applause
when we make a right decision,
just a calm sense of resolution and peace.

Gloria Gaither

Never support an experience which does not
have God as its source, and faith
in God as its result.

Oswald Chambers

God's sovereignty is a reality,
and man's responsibility is a reality too.

J. I. Packer

Don't worry about what you do not
understand.... Worry about what you do
understand in the Bible but do not live by.

Corrie ten Boom

Today's Prayer

Lord, this world has countless
distractions, interruptions and
frustrations. When I take my eye
away from You and Your Word, I suffer.
But when I turn my thoughts, my faith,
my trust, and my prayers to You,
Lord, You guide my path. Let me live
righteously according to Your
commandments and let me discover
Your will and follow Your Word
this day and always.

Amen

A Prayer for the Journey... God's Love

For I am persuaded, that neither death, nor life, nor angels, nor principalities, nor powers, nor things present, nor things to come, nor height, nor depth, nor any other creature, shall be able to separate us from the love of God, which is in Christ Jesus our Lord.

Romans 8:38-39 KJV

God loves you. Period. He loves you more than you can imagine; His affection is deeper and more profound than you can fathom. God made you in His own image and gave you salvation through the person of His Son Jesus Christ. And now, precisely because you are a wondrous creation treasured by God, a question presents itself: What will you do in response to God's love? Will you ignore it or embrace it? Will you return it or neglect it? The decision, of course, is yours and yours alone.

When you embrace God's love, you are forever changed. When you embrace God's love, you feel differently about yourself, your neighbors, and your world. More importantly, you share God's message—and His love—with others.

As you begin the next phase of your life, accept the eternal graduation gift: God's love for you. Through His Son, God offers his love freely. Accept it. Today.

For God so loved the world that he gave
his one and only Son, that whoever believes in
him shall not perish but have eternal life.

John 3:16 NIV

God proved his love on the cross.

Billy Graham

On the whole, God's love for us is a much safer
subject to think about than our love for him.
Nobody can always have devout feelings; and
even if we could, feelings are not what God
principally cares about. Christian love,
either toward God or toward man, is an
affair of the will. But the great thing to
remember is that, though our feelings
come and go, his love for us does not.

C. S. Lewis

Knowing God's sovereignty and unconditional
love imparts a beauty to life…
and to you.

Kay Arthur

Today's Prayer

Thank you, Lord, for Your love.
Your love is boundless, infinite, and
eternal. Today, let me pause and reflect
upon Your love for me, and let me share
that love with all those who cross my
path. As an expression of my love for
You, Lord, let me share the saving message of Your Son Jesus with a world in
desperate need of His peace.

Amen

8

A Prayer for the Journey... Perseverance

Let us run with patience the race that is set before us, looking unto Jesus the author and finisher of our faith; who for the joy that was set before him endured the cross, despising the shame, and is set down at the right hand of the throne of God.

Hebrews 12:1-2 KJV

Now that you've graduated, the hard work is over…right? Wrong! Even if you have worked *very* hard in school, there is still more work to do…much more work. In fact, the most challenging years of your life are probably still ahead, so prepare yourself. And learn to be patient.

Our savior, Christ Jesus, finished what He began. Despite the torture He endured, despite the shame of the cross, Jesus was steadfast in His faithfulness to God. We, too, must remain faithful, especially during times of hardship and pain.

Perhaps you are in a hurry for God to reveal His plans for your life. If so, be forewarned: God operates on His own timetable, not yours. Sometimes, God may answer your prayers with silence, and when He does, you must patiently persevere. In times of trouble, seek God through prayer and lean upon His strength. Whatever your problem, He can handle it. Your job is to keep persevering until He does.

Stand still and refuse to retreat. Look at it
as God looks at it and draw upon his power.

Chuck Swindoll

I learned as never before that persistent calling
upon the Lord breaks through every stronghold
of the devil, for nothing is impossible with God.
For Christians in these troubled times,
there is simply no other way.

Jim Cymbala

Keep adding, keep walking, keep advancing;
do not stop, do not turn back, do not turn
from the straight road.

St. Augustine

For you have need of endurance, so that when
you have done the will of God,
you may receive what was promised.

Hebrews 10:36 NASB

Today's Prayer

Lord, sometimes this life is difficult
indeed. Sometimes, we are burdened
or fearful. Sometimes, we cry tears
of bitterness or loss, but even then,
You never leave our sides. Today, Lord,
let me be a finisher of my faith.
Let me persevere—even if the day is
difficult—and let me follow Your Son
Jesus Christ this day and forever.

Amen

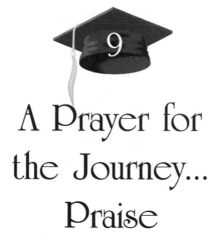

A Prayer for
the Journey...
Praise

I will praise the name of God with a
song, and will magnify him with
thanksgiving.

Psalm 69:30 KJV

When is the best time to praise God? In church? Before dinner is served? When we tuck little children into bed? None of the above. The best time to praise God is all day, every day, to the greatest extent we can, with thanksgiving in our hearts, and with a song on our lips.

Too many of us, even well-intentioned believers, tend to divide our waking hours into a few familiar categories: work, rest, play, family time, and worship. To do so is a mistake. Worship and praise should be woven into the fabric of everything we do; it should never be relegated to a weekly three-hour visit to church on Sunday morning.

Theologian Wayne Oates once admitted, "Many of my prayers are made with my eyes open. You see, it seems I'm always praying about something, and it's not always convenient—or safe—to close my eyes." Dr. Oates understood that God *always* hears our prayers and that the relative position of our eyelids is of little concern to Him.

Today, find more time to lift your concerns to God in prayer, and praise Him for all that He has done. Whether your eyes are open or closed, He's listening.

Praise and thank God for who He is
and for what He has done for you.

Billy Graham

If you will not worship God seven days a week,
you do not worship Him on one day a week.

A. W. Tozer

Dear God, preoccupy my thoughts with
your praise beginning today.

Joni Eareckson Tada

O praise the LORD, all ye nations: praise him,
all ye people. For his merciful kindness
is great toward us: and the truth of the LORD
endureth for ever. Praise ye the LORD.

Psalm 117:1-2 KJV

Today's Prayer

Lord, Your hand created the smallest grain of sand and the grandest stars in the heavens. You watch over Your entire creation, and You watch over me. Thank You, Lord, for loving this world so much that You sent your Son to die for our sins. Let me always be grateful for the priceless gift of Your Son, and let me praise Your holy name forever.

Amen

A Prayer for
the Journey...
Talents

Now there are varieties of gifts,
but the same Spirit. And there
are varieties of ministries,
and the same Lord.

1 Corinthians 12:4-5 NASB

All of us have special talents, and you are no exception. But your talent is no guarantee of success; it must be cultivated and nurtured; otherwise, it will go unused…and God's gift to you will be squandered.

In the 25th chapter of Matthew, Jesus tells the "Parable of the Talents." In it, He describes a master who leaves his servants with varying amounts of money (talents). When the master returns, some servants have put their money to work and earned more, to which the master responds, *Well done, good and faithful servant! You have been faithful with a few things; I will put you in charge of many things. Come and share your master's happiness! (Matthew 25:21 NIV)*

But the story does not end so happily for the foolish servant who was given a single talent but did nothing with it. For this man, the master has nothing but reproach: *You wicked, lazy servant…. (Matthew 25:26 NIV)* The message from Jesus is clear: We must use our talents, not waste them.

Your particular talent is a treasure on temporary loan from God. He intends that your talents enrich the world and enrich your life. Value the gift that God has given you, nourish it, make it grow, and share it with the world. Then, when you meet *your* Master face-to-face, you, too, will hear those wonderful words, "Well done, good and faithful servant!…Come and share your Master's happiness!"

One thing taught large in the Holy Scriptures
is that while God gives His gifts freely, He will
require a strict accounting of them at the end
of the road. Each man is personally responsible
for his store, be it large or small, and will be
required to explain his use of it before the
judgment seat of Christ.

A. W. Tozer

Employ whatever God has entrusted you with,
in doing good, all possible good, in every
possible kind and degree....

John Wesley

You are the only person on earth
who can use your ability.

Zig Ziglar

Neglect not the gift that is in thee....

I Timothy 4:14 KJV

Today's Prayer

Lord, You have given all of us talents,
and I am no different. You have blessed
me with a gift—let me discover it,
nurture it, and use it to the glory of
Your Kingdom. Today, let me be
a good and faithful steward, Lord,
of my talents and possessions. And,
let me give the glory to You as
I share the Good News of Your Son,
Christ Jesus.

Amen

11

A Prayer for the Journey... God's Support

The LORD is my shepherd; I shall not want. He maketh me to lie down in green pastures: he leadeth me beside the still waters. He restoreth my soul: he leadeth me in the paths of righteousness for his name's sake. Yea, though I walk through the valley of the shadow of death, I will fear no evil: for thou art with me; thy rod and thy staff they comfort me. Thou preparest a table before me in the presence of mine enemies: thou anointest my head with oil; my cup runneth over. Surely goodness and mercy shall follow me all the days of my life: and I will dwell in the house of the LORD for ever.

Psalm 23:1-6 KJV

Open your Bible to its center, and you'll find the Book of Psalms. In it are some of the most beautiful words ever translated into the English language, with none more beautiful than the 23rd Psalm. David describes God as being like a shepherd who cares for His flock. No wonder these verses have provided comfort and hope to generations of believers.

You are precious in the eyes of God. You are His priceless creation, made in His image, and protected by Him. God watches over every step you make and every breath you take, so you need never be afraid. But sometimes, fear has a way of slipping into the minds and hearts of even the most devout believers.

On occasion, you will confront circumstances that trouble you to the very core of your soul. When you are afraid, trust in God. When you are worried, turn your concerns over to Him. When you are anxious, be still and listen for the quiet assurance of God's promises. And then, place your life in His hands. He is your shepherd today and throughout eternity. Trust the Shepherd.

When you have no helpers, see all your helpers
in God. When you have many helpers,
see God in all your helpers. When you have
nothing but God, see all in God; when you have
everything, see God in everything. Under all
conditions, stay thy heart only on the Lord.

C. H. Spurgeon

We have ample evidence that the Lord is able
to guide. The promises cover every imaginable
situation. All we need to do is to take
the hand he stretches out.

Elisabeth Elliot

If we are beset by an unseen foe, we are also
befriended by an Unseen Friend. Great is our
adversary, but greater is our ally.

Vance Havner

Come unto me, all ye that labor and
are heavy laden, and I will give you rest.

Matthew 11:28 KJV

Today's Prayer

Lord, You are my shepherd.
You care for me; You love me; You
protect me. With You as my shield,
I have no reason ever to be afraid.
But sometimes, Lord, I *am* afraid. In
times of uncertainty, I feel threatened.
In times of sorrow, I weep. In times
of trouble, I become angry. Help me,
Lord, to lean not upon my own
incomplete understanding, but upon
You. Keep me ever-mindful of Your
promises, and let me trust You always.
You are my shepherd, Lord;
and I am Yours forever.

Amen

12

A Prayer for the Journey... Generosity

Let us not lose heart in doing good, for in due time we will reap if we do not grow weary. So then, while we have opportunity, let us do good to all people, and especially to those who are of the household of the faith.

Galatians 6:9-10 NASB

In Paul's second letter to the Corinthians, he reminds us that "God loves a cheerful giver." *(9:7 NIV)* These words are as relevant today as they were the day that Paul penned them. God's work on earth is done, in part, by those of us who have chosen to give our lives to His Son Jesus. God works in us and through us; we are His servants and He is our loving Master. The Master's commandment is clear: Give generously and cheerfully…and then keep giving generously and cheerfully.

Today, look for opportunities to give and to serve. When you look carefully, you need not look far: Those in need are all around us.

We can share our possessions, our time, or our prayers. We can help the family next door or the family halfway around the globe. We can give the gift of love, or we can extend the hand of friendship. However we choose to give—whenever we choose to give—we live according to the Master's plan.

But this I say, He which soweth sparingly shall
reap also sparingly; and he which soweth
bountifully shall reap also bountifully. Every man
according as he purposeth in his heart, so let him
give; not grudgingly, or of necessity: for God
loveth a cheerful giver.

II Corinthians 9:6-7 KJV

Since you cannot do good to all, you are to pay
special regard to those who, by the accidents of
time, or place, or circumstances, are brought
into closer connection with you.

St. Augustine

We are never more like God than when we give.

Chuck Swindoll

It is the duty of every Christian to be Christ
to his neighbor.

Martin Luther

Today's Prayer

Lord, You have blessed with me
a love that is far beyond my limited
understanding. You loved me before
I was ever born; You sent Your Son
Jesus to redeem me from my sins;
You have given me the gift of eternal life.
Let me be thankful always, and let me
praise You always. Today, let me share
priceless blessings I have received:
Let me share my joy, my possessions,
and my faith with others. And, let me be
a humble giver, Lord, so that all the
glory might be Yours.

Amen

A Prayer for
the Journey...
Hard Work

Whatever your hand finds to do, do
it with all your might....
Ecclesiastes 9:10 NIV

Now that graduation is a not-too-distant-memory, it's time to celebrate…for awhile. Then, it's time to move on to your next grand adventure. Wherever that adventure may lead, be forewarned: Success will depend, in large part, upon the quality and quantity of your work.

God's Holy Word commends the value and importance of hard work. In his second letter to the Thessalonians, Paul warns, " …if any would not work, neither should he eat." *(3:10 KJV)* And the Book of Proverbs proclaims, "One who is slack in his work is brother to one who destroys." *(18:9 NIV)* In short, God has created a world in which diligence is rewarded and sloth is not. So whatever it is that you choose to do, do it with commitment, excitement, and vigor.

Hard work is not simply a proven way to get ahead, it's also part of God's plan for you. God did not create you for a life of mediocrity; He created you for far greater things. Reaching for greater things usually requires work and lots of it, which is perfectly fine with God. After all, He knows that you're up to the task, and He has big plans for you. Very big plans…

We trust as if it all depended on God,
and work as if it all depended on us.

C. H. Spurgeon

Work, work, from early until late. In fact,
I have so much to do that I shall spend
the first three hours in prayer.

Martin Luther

Ordinary work, which is what most of us do
most of the time, is ordained by God
every bit as much as is the extraordinary.

Elisabeth Elliot

But let every man prove his own work, and
then shall he have rejoicing in himself alone,
and not in another. For every man shall bear
his own burden.

Galatians 6:4-5 KJV

Today's Prayer

Lord, I know that You desire a
bountiful harvest for all Your children.
But You have instructed us that we
must sow *before* we reap, not after.
Help me, Lord, to sow the seeds of
Your abundance everywhere I go.
Let me be diligent in all my
undertakings and give me patience
to wait for Your harvest. In time,
Lord, let me reap the harvest that
is found in Your will for my life.

Amen

A Prayer for
the Journey...
Worry

For this reason I say to you, do not
be worried about your life, *as to* what
you will eat or what you will drink;
nor for your body, *as to* what you will
put on. Is not life more than food,
and the body more than clothing?
Look at the birds of the air, that
they do not sow, nor reap nor gather
into barns, and *yet* your heavenly
Father feeds them. Are you not
worth much more than they?

Matthew 6:25-26 NASB

Because we are fallible human beings, we worry. Even though we, as Christians, have the assurance of salvation—even though we, as Christians, have the promise of God's love and protection—we find ourselves fretting over the countless details of everyday life. Jesus understood our concerns when he spoke the reassuring words found in the sixth chapter of Matthew.

Perhaps you are concerned about the inevitable changes that have come as a result of your graduation. Perhaps you are uncertain about your future or your finances. Or, perhaps you are simply a "worrier" by nature. If so, make the sixth chapter of Matthew a regular part of your daily Bible reading. This beautiful passage will remind you that God still dwells in His heaven and you are His beloved child. Then, perhaps, you will worry a little less and trust God a little more. And, that's as it should be because God is trustworthy…and you are protected.

Because God is my sovereign Lord, I was not worried. He manages perfectly, day and night, year in and year out, the movements of the stars, the wheeling of the planets, the staggering coordination of events that goes on at the molecular level in order to hold things together. There is no doubt that he can manage the timing of my days and weeks.

Elisabeth Elliot

The LORD himself goes before you and will be with you; he will never leave you nor forsake you. Do not be afraid; do not be discouraged.

Deuteronomy 31:8 NIV

Any concern too small to be turned into a prayer is too small to be made into a burden.

Corrie ten Boom

Pray, and let God worry.

Martin Luther

Today's Prayer

Lord, You sent Your Son to live
as a man on this earth, and You know
what it means to be completely human.
You understand my worries and fears,
Lord, and You forgive me when I am
weak. When my faith begins to wane,
Help me, Lord, to trust You more. Let
my trust in Your promises overcome my
worries and my doubts. Then, with Your
Holy Word on my lips and with the love
of Your Son in my heart, let me live
courageously, faithfully, prayerfully, and
thankfully today and every day.

Amen

A Prayer for the Journey... Kindness

> The merciful man does himself
> good, but the cruel man does
> himself harm.
>
> *Proverbs 11:17 NASB*

In the busyness and confusion of daily life, it is easy to lose focus, and it easy to become frustrated. We are imperfect human beings struggling to manage our lives as best we can, but we often fall short. When we are distracted or disappointed, we may neglect to share a kind word or a kind deed. This oversight hurts others, but it hurts *us* most of all.

Kindness is God's commandment. Matthew 25:40 warns, …*Verily I say unto you, Inasmuch as ye have done it unto one of the least of these my brethren, ye have done it unto me. (KJV)* When we extend the hand of friendship to those who need it most, God promises His blessings. When we ignore the needs of others—or mistreat them—we risk God's retribution.

Today, slow yourself down and be alert for those who need your smile, your kind words, or your helping hand. Make kindness a centerpiece of your dealings with others. They will be blessed and you will be, too. When you offer a heaping helping of encouragement and hope to the world, you can't help getting a little bit on yourself.

Do all the good you can.
        By all the means you can.
        In all the ways you can.
        In all the places you can.
        At all the times you can.
        To all the people you can.
        As long as ever you can.

John Wesley

What is your focus today? Joy comes when
        it is Jesus first, others second...
            then you.

Kay Arthur

The good man brings good things out of
        the good stored up in him, and the evil man
            brings evil things out of the evil
                stored up in him.

Matthew 12:35 NIV

In everything, therefore, treat people the same
        way you want them to treat you,
        for this is the Law and the Prophets.

Matthew 7:12 NASB

Today's Prayer

Lord, sometimes this world can become a place of busyness, frustration, and confusion. Slow me down, Lord, that I might see the needs of those around me. Today, help me to show mercy on those in need. Today, let me spread kind words of thanksgiving and celebration in honor of Your Son. Today, let forgiveness rule my heart. And every day, Lord, let my love for Christ be reflected through deeds of kindness for those who need the healing touch of the Master's hand.

Amen

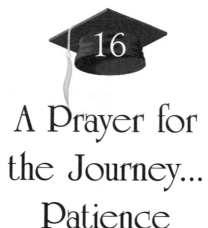

A Prayer for
the Journey...
Patience

The Lord is good to those whose
hope is in him, to the one who seeks
him; it is good to wait quietly for the
salvation of the Lord.

Lamentations 3:25-27 NIV

You've a graduate! And, now you are ready to move on with life. You have important things to do and important places to go, and if you're like most people, you're in a hurry to arrive. Congratulations: Your impatience means that you're energetic, enthused, and highly motivated. But a word of caution: God's world unfolds according to *His* timetable, not yours. So you'll be wise to develop the habits of hoping fervently, praying faithfully, and working patiently.

Patience can be a difficult skill to master especially if you're accustomed to life on a schedule. In school, your progress seems marked by semesters, by promotions, and, ultimately, by graduation. But life beyond the halls of academia is often different. Class isn't convened every morning at 8:00, and school isn't dismissed at 3:30. Rewards may not come as regularly as A's on a report card. Sometimes, your dreams will come true, and sometimes they won't. When they don't, be patient.

God has a magnificent plan for your life, and He is working—with you—to make that plan a reality. His plan is unfolding according to *His* infinite wisdom and in *His* own time. So keep praying, keep seeking God's will, and be patient. God is never in a rush, but He is always on time.

78

God is never in a hurry.

Oswald Chambers

Patience is the companion of wisdom.

St. Augustine

God never hurries. There are no deadlines
against which He must work. To know this
is to quiet our spirits and relax our nerves.

A. W. Tozer

Wait patiently on the Lord. Be brave and
courageous. Yes, wait patiently on the Lord.

Psalm 27:14 NLT

Today's Prayer

Lord, I seek Your will for my life,
but I also have hopes and dreams
of my own. I know, Lord, that the
universe unfolds according to Your plan
and Your timetable, not mine. But I am
waiting, Lord, and waiting can be
difficult. Give me patience and faith in
Your divine will. When I am frustrated,
let me rest in Your peace. When I am
disappointed, help me understand that
You always answer My prayers in
the infinity of Your wisdom, not the
urgency of my impatience. And in all
things, let me be thankful for the power
of Your love and the certainty
of Your promises.

Amen

A Prayer for
the Journey...
God's Presence

Be strong and courageous!
Do not tremble or be dismayed,
for the Lord your God is with
you wherever you go.

Joshua 1:9 NASB

He Is Here...

Are you tired? Discouraged? Fearful?
    Be comforted. God is with you.
Are you worried or anxious?
    Be confident in God's power.
    He will never desert you.
Do you see no hope for the future?
    Be courageous and call upon God.
    He will protect you and then
    use you according to His purposes.
Are you grieving? Know that God hears
    your cries. He will comfort you and,
    in time, He will dry your tears.
Are you confused? Listen to the quiet voice
    of your Heavenly Father.
    He is not a God of confusion.
Are you bitter? Talk with God
    and seek His guidance.
    He is a God of forgiveness.
Are you happy? Are you celebrating
    a great victory? Thank God and
    praise Him. He is the Giver
    of all things good.
In whatever condition you find yourself,
    wherever you are, whether you are happy
    or sad, victorious or vanquished, troubled
    or triumphant, celebrate God's presence.
And be comforted. God is not just near.
    He is here.

Criswell Freeman

The Lord Almighty is here among us;
  the God of Israel is our fortress. Come see the
    glorious works of the Lord....

Psalm 46:7-8 NLT

We need never shout across the spaces to
  an absent God. He is nearer than our own soul,
    closer than our most secret thoughts.

A. W. Tozer

God walks with us....He scoops us up in
His arms or simply sits with us in silent strength
until we cannot avoid the awesome recognition
    that yes, even now, He is here.

Gloria Gaither

If only we would stop lamenting and look up,
    God is here. Christ is risen.
The Spirit has been poured out from on high.

A. W. Tozer

Today's Prayer

Dear God, You are nearer to me
than the air that I breathe. Help me
to feel Your presence, Lord, in every
situation and in every circumstance.
You are with me, Lord, in times of
celebration and in times of sorrow.
You are with me when I am strong
and when I am weak. You never leave
my side, even when it seems to me
that You are far away. Today and
every day, Dear God, let me feel
You and acknowledge Your presence
because You are with me always.

Amen

18

A Prayer for the Journey... Thanksgiving

Make a joyful noise unto the Lord all ye lands. Serve the lord with gladness: come before his presence with singing. Know ye that the Lord he is God: it is he that hath made us, and not we ourselves; we are his people and the sheep of his pasture. Enter into his gates with thanksgiving, and into his courts with praise; be thankful unto him and bless his name. For the Lord is good; his mercy is everlasting; and his truth endureth to all generations.

Psalm 100:1-5 KJV

As believing Christians, we are blessed beyond measure. God sent his only Son to die for our sins. God has given us the priceless gifts of eternal love and eternal life. We, in turn, are instructed to approach our Heavenly Father with reverence and thanksgiving. But, sometimes, in the crush of everyday living, we simply don't stop long enough to pause and thank our Creator for the countless blessings He has bestowed upon us.

When we slow down and express our gratitude to the One who made us, we enrich our own lives and the lives of those around us. Thanksgiving should become a habit, a regular part of our daily routines. Yes, God has blessed us beyond measure, and we owe Him everything, including our eternal praise. To paraphrase the familiar children's blessing, "God is great, God is good, let us thank Him for…everything!"

In everything give thanks; for this is God's will
for you in Christ Jesus.

I Thessalonians 5:18 NIV

We ought to give thanks for all fortune:
if it is good, because it is good, if bad,
because it works in us patience, humility and
the contempt of this world and the hope of
our eternal country.

C. S. Lewis

It is good to give thanks to the Lord, to sing
praises to the Most High. It is good to
proclaim your unfailing love in the morning,
your faithfulness in the evening.

Psalm 92:2-3 NLT

It is only with gratitude that life becomes rich.

Dietrich Bonhoeffer

Today's Prayer

Heavenly Father, Your gifts
are greater than I can imagine,
and Your love for me is greater than
I can fathom. May I live each day with
thanksgiving in my heart and praise on
my lips. Thank You, Lord, for the gift of
Your Son and for the promise of eternal
life. Let me share the joyous news of
Jesus Christ with a world that
desperately needs His healing
touch this day and every day.

Amen

A Prayer for the Journey... Honesty

...and put on the new self, which in *the likeness of* God has been created in righteousness and holiness of the truth. Therefore, laying aside falsehood, speak truth each one of you with his neighbor, for we are members of one another.

Ephesians 4:24-25 NASB

It has been said on many occasions and in many ways that honesty is the *best* policy. For believers, it is far more important to note that honesty is *God's* policy. And, if we are to be servants worthy of our savior Jesus Christ, we must be honest and forthright in our communications with others.

Sometimes, honesty is difficult; sometimes, honesty is painful; always, honesty is God's commandment. In the Book of Exodus, God did not command, "Thou shalt not bear false witness when it is convenient." And he didn't say, "Thou shalt not bear false witness most of the time." God said, "Thou shalt not bear false witness against thy neighbor." Period.

Sometime soon, perhaps even today, you will be tempted to bend the truth or perhaps even break it. Resist that temptation. Truth is God's way…and it must also be yours.

A little lie is like a little pregnancy:
It doesn't take long before everyone knows.

C. S. Lewis

Integrity is not a given factor in everyone's life.
It is a result of self-discipline, inner trust,
and a decision to be relentlessly honest in all
situations in our lives.

John Maxwell

The man of integrity walks securely,
but he who takes crooked paths
will be found out.

Proverbs 10:9 NIV

Therefore, seeing we have this ministry,
as we have received mercy, we faint not;
but have renounced the hidden things of
dishonesty, not walking in craftiness,
nor handling the word of God deceitfully; but,
by manifestation of the truth, commending
ourselves to every man's conscience in
the sight of God.

II Corinthians 4:1 KJV

Today's Prayer

Heavenly Father, You instruct Your children to seek truth and to live righteously. Help me always to live according to Your commandments. Sometimes, Lord, speaking the truth is difficult, but let me always speak truthfully and forthrightly. And let me walk righteously and courageously so that others might see Your Grace reflected in my words and my deeds.

Amen

A Prayer for the Journey... Forgiveness

You have heard it said, "Love your neighbor and hate your enemy." But I tell you: Love your enemies and pray for those who persecute you, that you may be sons of your father in heaven.

Matthew 5:43-45 NIV

It has been said that life is an exercise in forgiveness. How true. Christ understood the importance of forgiveness when he commanded, "Love your enemies and pray for those who persecute you." But sometimes, forgiveness is difficult indeed.

When we have been injured or embarrassed, we feel the urge to strike back and to hurt the one who has hurt us. Christ instructs us to do otherwise. Believers are taught that forgiveness is God's way and that mercy is an integral part of God's plan for our lives. In short, we are commanded to weave the thread of forgiveness into the very fabric of our lives.

Today, as you go about your daily affairs, remember that *you* have already been forgiven by your heavenly Father, and so, too, should you forgive others. If you bear bitterness against anyone, take your bitterness to God and leave it there. If you are angry, pray for God's healing hand to calm your spirit. If you are troubled by some past injustice, read God's word and remember His commandment to forgive. When you follow that commandment and sincerely forgive those who have hurt you, you'll discover that a heavy burden has been lifted from your shoulders. And you'll discover that although forgiveness is indeed difficult, with God's help, all things are possible.

Whenever you stand praying, forgive,
if you have anything against anyone, so
that your Father in heaven will also forgive you
your transgressions.

Mark 11:25 NASB

Forgiveness is God's command.

Martin Luther

As you have received the mercy of God
by the forgiveness of sin and the promise
of eternal life, thus you must show mercy.

Billy Graham

There is no use in talking as if forgiveness
were easy....I could say of a certain man,
"Have I forgiven him more times than I can
count?" For we find that the work of forgiveness
has to be done over and over again.

C. S. Lewis

Today's Prayer

Heavenly Father, I know
that forgiveness is Your commandment,
but genuine forgiveness is difficult
indeed. I feel the strong desire to
strike out at those who have hurt me,
but You command me to refrain from
bitterness and to turn away from
revenge. Help me to Forgive others,
Lord, just as You have forgiven me. And,
keep me mindful, Dear God, that I am
never fully liberated until I have been
freed from the prison of hatred…and
that You offer freedom from that prison
through the person of Your Son, Jesus
Christ.

Amen

A Prayer for
the Journey...
Discipline

> He who tills his land will have plenty
> of food, but he who follows empty
> pursuits will have poverty in plenty.
> *Proverbs 28:19 NASB*

Students everywhere understand the profound sense of joy that accompanies two little words: "School's out!" In a brief, two-word exclamatory sentence, so much is said. "School's out!" means no more homework, no more papers, no more grades, and no more standardized tests. "School's out!" means it's time for a much-needed break from the daily grind. "School's out!" means it's time to put the books—and the worries—away. But before the celebration gets out of hand, be forewarned: "School's out!" does not mean that our work is done. To the contrary, the *real* work is probably just beginning.

Those who study and believe the Bible are confronted again and again with God's intention that His children lead disciplined lives. God doesn't reward laziness. Rather, He expects believers to adopt a disciplined approach to their lives. In Proverbs 28:19, the message is clear: work diligently and consistently, and then expect a bountiful harvest. But, never expect the harvest to precede the labor.

As a graduate, you've earned the right to proclaim "School's out!" at the top of your lungs. But, when all the shouting is over, remember that God rewards discipline just as certainly as He punishes indolence. And, if you're not sure what the word indolence means, your dictionary in that stack of books over there in the corner. Happy reading!

Let us not cease to do the utmost,
that we may incessantly go forward
in the way of the Lord; and let us not despair
of the smallness of our accomplishments.

John Calvin

All rising to a great place is by a winding stair.

Francis Bacon

The plans of the diligent lead to profit as
surely as haste leads to poverty.

Proverbs 21:5 NIV

The alternative to discipline is disaster.

Vance Havner

Today's Prayer

Dear Lord, Your Holy Word tells us
that You expect Your children to be
diligent and disciplined. You have told us
that the fields are ripe and the workers
are few. Lead me to Your fields, Lord,
and make me a disciplined worker in
service of Your Son, Christ Jesus.
When I am weary, give me strength.
When I am discouraged, give me hope.
Make me a disciplined, courageous,
industrious servant for Your Kingdom
today and forever.

Amen

A Prayer for the Journey... Humility

For whosoever exalteth himself shall be abased; and he that humbleth himself shall be exalted.

Luke 14:11 KJV

Dietrich Bonhoeffer observed, "It is very easy to overestimate the importance of our own achievements in comparison with what we owe others." How true. Even those of us who consider ourselves "self-made" men and women are deeply indebted to more people than we can count. Our first and greatest indebtedness, of course, is to God and His only begotten Son. But, we are also indebted to ancestors, parents, teachers, friends, spouses, family members, coworkers, fellow believers…and the list goes on.

With so many people who rightfully deserve to share the credit for our successes, how can we gloat? The answer, of course, is that we should not. Proverbs 16:18 warns us that *Pride goes before destruction….* *(NIV)* And 1 Peter 5:5 teaches us that *God opposes the proud but gives grace to the humble. (NIV)*

As a recent graduate, you have successfully completed an important chapter in your life. You are entitled to take pride in your accomplishments. But not *too much* pride. Instead of puffing out your chest and saying, "Look at me!", give credit where credit is due, starting with God. And rest assured: There is *no such thing* as a self-made man. All of us are made by God…and He deserves the glory.

Do you wish to be great? Then begin by being humble. Do you desire to construct a vast and lofty fabric? Think first about the foundation of humility. The higher your structure is to be, the deeper must be its foundation.

St. Augustine

The holy man is the most humble man you can meet.

Oswald Chambers

We must always speak of the efficacy of the ministry in such a manner that the entire praise of the work may be reserved for God alone.

John Calvin

Jesus had a humble heart. If He abides in us, pride will never dominate our lives.

Billy Graham

Today's Prayer

Heavenly Father, it is the nature of mankind to be prideful, and I am no exception. When I am boastful, Lord, keep me mindful that all my gifts come from You. When I feel prideful, remind me that You sent Your Son to be a humble carpenter and that Jesus was ridiculed and crucified on a cross. Let me grow beyond my need for earthly praise, God, and let me look only to You for approval. You are the Giver of all things good; let me give all the glory to You.

Amen

A Prayer for
the Journey...
Trusting God

The LORD is my rock, and my
fortress, and my deliverer; my God,
my strength, in whom I will trust….

Psalm 18:2 KJV

The little sign behind the cash register is yellow and frayed, but it still conveys a humorous, straightforward message: "In God we trust…all others pay cash!" As believers in Christ, we are called upon to agree with the *first* half of the shopkeeper's message: "In God we trust…."

Sometimes, because we are imperfect human beings who are afraid to trust God completely, we want absolute guarantees *before* we deliver the goods. But it doesn't work that way. Before we can expect God to work miracles in our lives, we must first trust Him with everything we have and everything we are. Then and only then will we begin to see the miraculous results of His endless love and His awesome power.

Do you aspire to do great things for God's kingdom? Then trust Him. Trust Him with every aspect of your life. Trust Him with your relationships. Trust Him with your finances. Follow His commandments and pray for His guidance. Then, wait patiently for God's revelations and for His blessings. In His own fashion and in His own time, God will bless you in ways that you could never have imagined.

Relying on God has to begin all over again
every day as if nothing had yet been done.

C. S. Lewis

Faith is unutterable trust in God, trust which
never dreams that He will not stand by us.

Oswald Chambers

Never be afraid to trust an unknown future
to a known God.

Corrie ten Boom

If we just give God the little that we have,
we can trust Him to make it go around.

Gloria Gaither

Today's Prayer

Lord, when I trust in things of this earth, I will be disappointed. But when I put my faith in You, I am secure. You are my rock and my shield. Upon your firm foundation I will build my life. When I am worried, Lord, let me trust in You. You will love me and protect me, and You will share Your boundless grace today, tomorrow, and forever.

Amen

24

A Prayer for
the Journey...
Encouraging Others

> But encourage one another day
> after day, as long as it is still called
> "Today," so that none of you will be
> hardened by the deceitfulness of sin.
>
> *Hebrews 3:13 NASB*

Life is a team sport, and all of us need occasional pats on the back from our teammates. As Christians, we are called upon to spread the Good News of Christ, and we are also called to spread a message of encouragement and hope to the world.

In the book of Ephesians, Paul writes, *Do not let any unwholesome talk come out of your mouths, but only what is helpful for building others up according to their needs, that it may benefit those who listen. (4:29 NIV)* Paul reminds us that when we choose our words carefully, we can have a powerful impact on those around us.

Whether you realize it or not, many people with whom you come in contact every day are in desperate need of a smile or an encouraging word. The world can be a difficult place, and countless friends and family members may be troubled by the challenges of everyday life. Since we don't always know who needs our help, the best strategy is to encourage all the people who cross our paths. So today, be a world-class source of encouragement to *everyone* you meet. Never has the need been greater.

Encouragement is the oxygen of the soul.

John Maxwell

Discouraged people don't need critics.
They hurt enough already. They don't need
more guilt or piled-on distress. They need
encouragement. They need a refuge.
A willing, caring, available someone.

Chuck Swindoll

We urge you, brethren, admonish the unruly,
encourage the fainthearted, help the weak,
be patient with everyone.

I Thessalonians 5:14 NASB

He climbs highest who helps another up.

Zig Ziglar

Today's Prayer

Dear Lord, You have loved me, cared for me, encouraged me, and saved me. Make me ever-grateful for Your grace. And just as You have lifted me up, let me also lift up others in a spirit of encouragement and hope. Today, let me share the healing message of Your Son, and in doing so, care for brothers and sisters in need. And to whatever extent I can be of service to others, Lord, may the glory be Yours.

Amen

A Prayer for the Journey... Renewal

I will give you a new heart and
put a new spirit in you....
Ezekiel 36:26 NIV

Even the most inspired Christians can, from time to time, find themselves running on empty. The demands of daily life can drain us of our strength and rob us of the joy that is rightfully ours in Christ. When we find ourselves tired, discouraged, or worse, there is a source from which we can draw the power needed to recharge our spiritual batteries. That source is God.

God intends that His children lead joyous lives filled with abundance and peace. But, sometimes, abundance and peace seem very far away. It is then that we must turn to God for renewal, and when we do, He will restore us.

Are you tired or troubled? Turn your heart toward God in prayer. Are you weak or worried? Take the time—or, more accurately, *make* the time—to delve deeply into God's Holy Word. Are you spiritually depleted? Call upon fellow believers to support you, and call upon Christ to renew your spirit and your life. When you do, you'll discover that the Creator of the universe stands always ready and always able to create a new sense of wonderment and joy in you.

Create in me a clean heart, O God;
and renew a right spirit within me.

Psalm 51:10 KJV

He stands fast as your rock, steadfast
as your safeguard, sleepless as your watcher,
valiant as your champion.

C. H. Spurgeon

He is the God of wholeness and restoration.

Stormie Omartian

Come to me all you who are weary and
burdened, and I will give you rest.
Take my yoke upon you and learn from me,
for I am gentle and humble in heart, and
you will find rest for your soul. For my yoke is
easy and my burden is light.

Matthew 11:28-30 NIV

Today's Prayer

Heavenly Father, sometimes
I am troubled, and sometimes, I grow
weary. When I am weak, Lord, give me
strength. When I am discouraged, renew
me. When I am fearful, let me feel Your
healing touch. Let me always trust in
Your promises, Lord, and let me draw
strength from those promises and from
Your unending love.

Amen

A Prayer for
the Journey...
Anger

Refrain from anger and turn
from wrath; do not fret —
it leads only to evil.

Psalm 37:8 NIV

Anger is a natural human emotion that is sometimes necessary and appropriate. Even Jesus became angry when confronted with the money changers in the temple: *And Jesus entered the temple and drove out all those who were buying and selling in the temple, and overturned the tables of the money changers and the seats of those who were selling doves.* *(Matthew 21:12 NASB)* Righteous indignation is an appropriate response to evil, but God does not intend that anger should rule our lives. Far from it. God intends that we turn away from anger whenever possible and forgive our neighbors just as we seek forgiveness for ourselves.

Life is full of frustrations: some great and some small. On occasion, you, like Jesus, will confront evil, and when you do, you may respond as He did: vigorously and without reservation. But more often, your frustrations will be of the more mundane variety. As long as you live here on earth, you will face countless opportunities to lose your temper over small, relatively insignificant events: a traffic jam, a spilled cup of coffee, an inconsiderate comment, a broken promise. When you are tempted to lose your temper over the minor inconveniences of life, don't. Turn away from anger, hatred, bitterness and regret. Turn instead to God. When you do, you'll be following His commandments *and* giving yourself a valuable gift…the gift of peace.

Don't sin by letting anger gain control over
you. Think about it overnight
and remain silent.

Psalm 4:4 NLT

Jesus had a forgiving and understanding heart.
If he lives within us, mercy will temper our
relationships with our fellow men.

Billy Graham

….do not let the sun go down on your anger,
and do not give the devil an opportunity.

Ephesians 4:26-27 NASB

Only the truly forgiven are truly forgiving.

C. S. Lewis

Today's Prayer

Lord, as a frail human being,
I can be quick to anger and slow to
forgive. But I know, Lord, that You
seek that I live in peace. When I fall
prey to pettiness, restore my sense of
perspective. When I fall prey to irrational
anger, give me inner calm. When I am
slow to forgive, Lord, keep me mindful of
Your commandment that I love my
neighbor as myself. Let me follow in the
footsteps of Your Son Jesus who forgave
His persecutors, and as I turn away from
anger, let me claim for myself the peace
that You intend for my life.

Amen

27

A Prayer for
the Journey...
Optimism

Finally, brethren, whatsoever things
are true, whatsoever things are
honest, whatsoever things are just,
whatsoever things are pure,
whatsoever things are lovely,
whatsoever things are of good report;
if there be any virtue, and if there be
any praise, think on these things.

Philippians 4:8 KJV

Now that your diploma is safely signed and framed, it's time to make plans for the next leg of your life's journey. And, as you make plans, remember that the quality of that journey will depend, in part, on the quality of your thoughts. If you allow yourself to fall into the unfortunate habit of negative thinking, you will bring needless suffering into your life. But, if you choose, instead, to follow the directive of Philippians 4:8, you will focus your attention upon "whatsoever things are true…honest…just…pure…lovely….and of good report." And your life will be richer for it.

So, the next time you find yourself dwelling upon the negatives of life, refocus your attention to things positive. The next time you find yourself falling prey to the blight of pessimism, stop yourself, turn your thoughts around, and give yourself the gift of optimism. And, if you see your glass as "half-empty," rest assured that your spiritual vision is impaired. With God, your glass is *never* half empty. With God as your protector and Christ as your Savior, your glass is filled to the brim and overflowing…forever.

Your attitude is more important
than your aptitude.

Zig Ziglar

Make the least of all that goes and the most
of all that comes. Don't regret what is past.
Cherish what you have. Look forward to all
that is to come. And most important of all,
rely moment by moment on Jesus Christ.

Gigi Graham Tchividjian

One hour in heaven, and we shall be ashamed
that we ever grumbled.

Vance Havner

Set your mind on the things above,
not on the things that are on earth.

Colossians 3:2 NASB

Today's Prayer

Lord, You care for me, You love me,
and You have given me the priceless gift
of eternal life through Your Son Jesus.
Because of You, Lord, I have every
reason to live each day with celebration
and hope. Help me to face this day with
a spirit of optimism and thanksgiving
so that I may lift the spirits of those
I meet just as certainly as I share the
Good News of Your Son. And, let me
focus my thoughts on You and
Your incomparable gifts
today and forever.

Amen

28

A Prayer for the Journey... Courage

The Lord is my light and my salvation; whom shall I fear? The Lord is the strength of my life; of whom shall I be afraid?

Psalm 27:1 KJV

Every human life is a tapestry of events: some grand, some not-so-grand, and some downright tragic. When we reach the mountaintops of life, praising God is easy. In the moment of triumph, we trust God's plan. But when the storm clouds form overhead and we find ourselves in the dark valley of despair, our faith is stretched, sometimes to the breaking point. As Christians, we can be comforted: Wherever we find ourselves, whether at the top of the mountain or the depths of the valley, God is there, and because He cares for us, we can live courageously.

Believing Christians have every reason to be courageous. After all, the ultimate battle has already been fought and won on the cross at Calvary. But even dedicated followers of Christ may find their courage tested by the inevitable disappointments and tragedies that occur in the lives of believers and non-believers alike.

The next time you find your courage tested to the limit, remember that God is as near as your next breath, and remember that He offers salvation to His children. He is your shield and your strength; He is your protector and your deliverer. Call upon Him in your hour of need and then be comforted. Whatever your challenge, whatever your trouble, God can handle it. And will.

Do not be afraid...I am your shield,
your very great reward.

Genesis 15:1 NIV

Down through the centuries, in times of trouble
and trial, God has brought courage to the hearts
of those who love Him. The Bible is filled with
assurances of God's help and comfort in every
kind of trouble which might cause fears to arise
in the human heart. You can look ahead with
promise, hope, and joy.

Billy Graham

Be strong and courageous, and do the work.
Do not be afraid or discouraged, for
the Lord God, my God, is with you.

I Chronicles 28:20 NIV

What is courage? It is the ability to be strong
in trust, in conviction, in obedience.
To be courageous is to step out in faith—
to trust and obey, no matter what.

Kay Arthur

Today's Prayer

Lord, sometimes I face challenges
that leave me breathless. When I am
fearful, let me lean upon You. Keep me
ever-mindful, Lord, that You are my
God, my strength, and my shield. With
You by my side, I have nothing to fear.
And with Your Son Jesus as my Savior,
I have received the priceless gift of
eternal life. Help me to be a grateful
and courageous servant this day
and every day.

Amen

A Prayer for
the Journey...
Abundance

I am come that they might have life,
and that they might have it more
abundantly.

John 10:10 KJV

The tenth Chapter of John tells us that Christ came to earth so that our lives might be filled with abundance. But what, exactly, did Jesus mean when He promised "life…more abundantly?" Was Jesus referring to material possessions or financial wealth? Hardly. When Jesus declared Himself the shepherd of mankind *(John 10:7-9)*, he offered a different kind of abundance: a spiritual richness that extends beyond the temporal boundaries of this world.

The fullness of life in Christ is available to all who seek it and claim it. Count yourself among that number. Seek first the salvation available through a personal relationship with Jesus Christ, and then claim the joy, the peace, and the spiritual abundance that the Shepherd offers His sheep.

God loves you and wants you to experience
    peace and life—abundant and eternal.
Billy Graham

I am holding you by your right hand—
    I, the Lord your God. And I say to you,
    "Do not be afraid. I am here to help you...."
Isaiah 41:13 NLT

The Lord is glad to open the gate to every
    knocking soul. It opens very freely; its hinges
    are not rusted, no bolts secure it. Have faith
and enter at this moment through holy courage.
    If you knock with a heavy heart, you shall yet
    sing with joy of spirit. Never be discouraged!
C. H. Spurgeon

Ask, and it shall be given you; seek, and
    ye shall find; knock, and it shall be opened
unto you: for every one that asketh receiveth;
    and he that seeketh findeth; and to him that
    knocketh it shall be opened.
Matthew 7:7-8 KJV

Today's Prayer

Lord, Thank You for the
abundant life that is mine through
Christ Jesus. Guide me according to
Your will, and help me to be a worthy
servant through all that I say and do.
Give me courage, Lord, to claim the
rewards You have promised, and when
I do, let all the glory be Yours.

Amen

A Prayer for the Journey... Love

But now faith, hope, love, abide
these three; but the greatest of
these is love.

I Corinthians 13:13 NASB

The familiar words of first Corinthians 13 remind us that love is God's commandment. Faith is important, of course. So, too, is hope. But, love is more important still.

Christ showed His love for us on the cross, and, as Christians, we are called upon to return Christ's love by sharing it. We are commanded (not advised, not encouraged…commanded!) to love one another just as Christ loved us. *(John 13:34)* That's a tall order, but as Christians, we are obligated to follow it.

Sometimes, love is easy (perhaps puppies and sleeping children come to mind) and sometimes love is hard (perhaps fallible human beings come to mind). But God's Word is clear: We are to love *all* our neighbors, not just the lovable ones. So, today, take time to spread Christ's message by word and by example. And the greatest of these is example.

He who is filled with love is filled with
God Himself.

St. Augustine

The whole being of any Christian is Faith
and Love.... Faith brings the man to God,
love brings him to men.

Martin Luther

Love is an attribute of God. To love others
is evidence of a genuine faith.

Kay Arthur

Love is the seed of all hope.
It is the enticement to trust, to risk,
to try, to go on.

Gloria Gaither

Today's Prayer

Lord, You have given me the gift
of eternal love; let me share that gift
with the world. Help me, Lord, to show
kindness to those who cross my path,
and let me show tenderness and
unfailing love to my family and friends.
Make me generous with words of
encouragement and praise. And,
help me always to reflect the love
that Christ Jesus gave me so that
through me, others might find Him.

Amen

A Prayer for
the Journey...
God's Plan

The steps of the Godly are directed
by the Lord. He delights in every
detail of their lives. Though they
stumble, they will not fall, for the
Lord holds them by the hand.

Psalm 37:23-24 NLT

God has plans for your life. Big plans. But He won't force you to follow His will; to the contrary, He has given you *free* will, the ability to make choices and decisions on your own. With the freedom to choose comes the responsibility of living with the consequences of the choices you make.

The most important decision of your life is, of course, your commitment to accept Jesus Christ as your personal Lord and Savior. And, once your eternal destiny is secured, you will undoubtedly ask yourself the question "What now, Lord?" If you earnestly seek God's will for your life, you will find it…in time.

Sometimes, God's plans are easily detected, but other times, He leads us through the wilderness before He delivers us to the Promised Land. So, be patient, keep searching, and keep praying. If you do, then in time, God will answer your prayers and make His plans known.

As you begin your life after graduation, study God's Word and be ever-watchful for His signs. Associate with fellow Christians who will encourage your spiritual growth, and listen to that inner voice that speaks to you in the quiet moments of your daily devotionals. God is here, and He intends to use you in wonderful, unexpected ways. Listen…He is here, even now.

138

God will not permit any troubles to come
upon us, unless He has a specific plan by
which great blessing can come out
of the difficulty.

Peter Marshall

God prepared a plan for your life alone—
and neither man nor the devil can
destroy that plan.

Kay Arthur

Even when we cannot see the why and
wherefore of God's dealings, we know that
there is love in and behind them, and
so we can rejoice always.

J. I. Packer

God possesses infinite knowledge and
awareness which is uniquely His. At all times,
even in the midst of any type of suffering,
I can realize that he knows, loves, watches,
understands, and more than that,
He has a purpose.

Billy Graham

Today's Prayer

Lord, You have a plan for my life
that is grander than I can imagine.
Let Your purposes be my purposes.
Let Your will be my will. When I am
confused, give me clarity. When I am
frightened, give me courage. Let me be
Your faithful servant, always seeking
Your guidance for my life. And,
let me always be a shining beacon
for Your Son Jesus today
and every day that I live.

Amen

More Bible Verses
for the Graduate's
Journey

Spiritual Abundance...

I am come that they might have life, and
that they might have it more abundantly.

John 10:10 KJV

Success, success to you, and success to those
who help you, for your God is with you....

I Chronicles 12:18 NIV

Have faith in the LORD your God and you
will be upheld; have faith in his prophets and
you will be successful.

II Chronicles 20:20 NIV

Thou wilt show me the path of life:
in thy presence is fulness of joy; at thy
right hand there are pleasures for evermore.

Psalm 16:11 KJV

Delight thyself also in the LORD; and
he shall give thee the desires of thine heart.

Psalm 37:4 KJV

142

Accepting Christ...

For God so loved the world, that he gave his
only begotten Son, that whosoever believeth in
him should not perish, but have everlasting life.

John 3:16 KJV

For the wages of sin is death, but the gift of
God is eternal life in Christ Jesus our Lord.

Romans 6:23 NIV

He saved us, not on the basis of deeds which
we have done in righteousness, but according
to His mercy, by the washing of regeneration
and renewing by the Holy Spirit, whom He
poured out upon us richly through
Jesus Christ our Savior....

Titus 3:5-6 NASB

Jesus answered and said unto her, Whosoever
drinketh of this water shall thirst again: but
whosoever drinketh of the water that I shall give
him shall never thirst; but the water that I shall
give him shall be in him a well of water springing
up into everlasting life.

John 4:13-14 KJV

In Times of Trouble,
God Stands Firm...

We are troubled on every side, yet
not distressed; we are perplexed, but not in
despair; persecuted, but not forsaken; cast down,
but not destroyed....

II Corinthians 4:8-9 KJV

They do not fear bad news; they confidently
trust the Lord to care for them.
They are confident and fearless and
can face their foes triumphantly.

Psalm 112: 7-8 NLT

Come to me all you who are weary and
burdened, and I will give you rest. Take
my yoke upon you and learn from me,
for I am gentle and humble in heart, and
you will find rest for your soul. For my yoke
is easy and my burden is light.

Matthew 11:28-30 NIV

Wait on the LORD: be of good courage,
and he shall strengthen thine heart:
wait, I say, on the LORD.

Psalm 27:14 KJV

144

God's Way...

Blessed is the man that walketh not in
    the counsel of the ungodly, nor standeth
    in the way of sinners, nor sitteth in
    the seat of the scornful.

Psalm 1:1 KJV

And you shall do what is good and right
    in the sight of the Lord, that it may be
    well with you....

Deuteronomy 6:18 NASB

Be not wise in thine own eyes:
    fear the Lord and depart from evil.

Proverbs 3:7 KJV

...Turn from your evil ways and keep
    My commandments, My statutes according
to all the law which I commanded your fathers....

II Kings: 17:13

...Abhor that which is evil;
    cleave to that which is good.

Romans 12:9 KJV

God's Timing...

There is a time for everything, and
a season for every activity under heaven....

Ecclesiastes 3:1 NIV

He has made everything beautiful in its time.
He has also set eternity in the hearts of men;
yet they cannot fathom what God
has done from beginning to end.

Ecclesiastes 3:11 NIV

...show me now your way, that I may know you,
that I may find grace in your sight.

Exodus 15:2 KJV

Trust the Lord your God with all your heart
and lean not on your own understanding;
in all your ways acknowledge him, and
he will make your paths straight.

Proverbs 3:5-6 NIV

And we know that in all things God works
for the good of those who love him, who have
been called according to his purpose.

Romans 8:28 NIV

Celebration...

This is the day the Lord has made;
  let us rejoice and be glad in it.
Psalm 118:24 NIV

A merry heart doeth good like a medicine:
  but a broken spirit drieth the bones.
Proverbs 17:22 KJV

A cheerful look brings joy to the heart,
  and good news gives health to the bones.
Proverbs 15:30 NIV

The Lord is king! Let the earth rejoice!
  Let the farthest islands be glad.
Psalm 97:1 NLT

...ye shall be sorrowful, but your sorrow
  shall be turned into joy.
John 16:20 KJV

With God by Our Sides, We Need Never Be Afraid...

For thou wilt light my candle:
   the LORD my God will enlighten my darkness.

Psalm 18:28 KJV

The Lord himself goes before you and
      will be with you; he will never leave you
         nor forsake you. Do not be afraid;
            do not be discouraged.

Deuteronomy 31:8 NIV

He replied, "You of little faith, why are you
   so afraid?" Then he got up and rebuked the
winds and the waves, and it was completely calm.

Matthew 8:26 NIV

Fear of man will prove to be a snare, but
   whoever trusts in the Lord is kept safe.

Proverbs 29:25 NIV

I sought the LORD, and he heard me, and
   delivered me from all my fears.

Psalm 34:4 KJV

Encouraging Others...

Take heed, brethren, lest there be in any of you
an evil heart of unbelief, in departing
from the living God. But exhort one another
daily, while it is called Today; lest any of you
be hardened through the deceitfulness of sin.

Hebrews 3:12-13 KJV

Do not let any unwholesome talk come out
of your mouths, but only what is helpful for
building others up according to their needs,
that it may benefit those who listen.

Ephesians 4:29 NIV

...let us consider how to stimulate
one another to love and good deeds.

Hebrews 10:24 KJV

We urge you, brethren, admonish the unruly,
encourage the fainthearted, help the weak,
be patient with everyone.

I Thessalonians 5:14 NASB

On Faith...

Surely goodness and mercy shall follow me
all the days of my life: and I will dwell in the
house of the Lord for ever.

Psalm 23:6 KJV

But he must ask in faith without any doubting,
for the one who doubts is like the surf
of the sea, driven and tossed by the wind.

James 1:6 NASB

Take therefore no thought for the morrow:
for the morrow shall take thought for
the things of itself. Sufficient unto
the day is the evil thereof.

Matthew 6:34 KJV

Be on the alert, stand firm in the faith,
act like men, be strong.

I Corinthians 16:13 NASB

For the Lord watches over the way of
the righteous, but the way
of the wicked will perish.

Psalm 1:6 NIV

God Calls Upon Us
to Forgive Others...

Be ye therefore merciful, as your Father
also is merciful.

Luke 6:36 KJV

A man's wisdom gives him patience;
it is to his glory to overlook an offense.

Proverbs 19:11 NIV

Then came Peter to him, and said, Lord,
how oft shall my brother sin against me, and
I forgive him? till seven times? Jesus saith unto
him, I say not unto thee, Until seven times: but,
Until seventy times seven.

Matthew 18:21-22 KJV

So in everything, do to others what you would
have them do to you, for this sums up
the Law and the Prophets.

Matthew 7:12 NIV

Blessed are the merciful: for they shall
obtain mercy.

Matthew 5:7 KJV

Using God's Gifts...

Neglect not the gift that is in thee....
I Timothy 4:14 KJV

His lord said unto him, Well done, thou good
and faithful servant: thou hast been faithful over
a few things, I will make thee ruler over many
things: enter thou into the joy of thy lord.
Matthew 25:21 KJV

Every good gift and every perfect gift is
from above, and cometh down from
the Father of lights.
James 1:17 KJV

I will thank you, Lord with all my heart;
I will tell of all the marvelous things you have
done. I will be filled with joy because of you.
I will sing praises to your name, O Most High.
Psalm 9: 1-2 NLT

Bless the LORD, O my soul, and
forget not all his benefits....
Psalm 103:2 KJV

God's Peace...

And let the peace of God rule in your hearts...
and be ye thankful.

Colossians 3:15 KJV

Be perfect, be of good comfort, be of one mind,
live in peace; and the God of love
and peace shall be with you.

II Corinthians 13:11 KJV

Return unto thy rest, O my soul;
for the LORD hath dealt bountifully with thee.

Psalm 116:7 KJV

Peace I leave with you, my peace I give unto
you: not as the world giveth, give I unto you.
Let not your heart be troubled,
neither let it be afraid.

John 14:27 KJV

God's Will...

Trust in the LORD with all thine heart; and
lean not unto thine own understanding.
In all thy ways acknowledge him, and
he shall direct thy paths.

Proverbs 3:5-6 KJV

And all things are of God, who hath reconciled
us to himself by Jesus Christ, and hath
given to us the ministry of reconciliation....

II Corinthians 5:18 KJV

Teach me to do thy will; for thou art my God:
thy Spirit is good; lead me into the
land of uprightness.

Psalm 143:10 KJV

For whosoever shall do the will of my Father
which is in heaven, the same is my brother,
and sister, and mother.

Matthew 12:50 KJV

Father, if it be possible, let this cup pass
from me: nevertheless, not as I will,
but as thou wilt.

Matthew 26:39 KJV

Patience…

And we desire that each one of you show
the same diligence so as to realize the full
assurance of hope until the end, so that you will
not be sluggish, but imitators of those who
through faith and patience inherit the promises.

Hebrews 6: 11-12 NASB

Better a patient man than a warrior, a man
who controls his temper than one
who takes a city.

Proverbs 16:32 NIV

Wait on the LORD: be of good courage,
and he shall strengthen thine heart:
wait, I say, on the LORD.

Psalm 27:14 KJV

…Those who wait upon the Lord,
they shall inherit the earth.

Psalm 37:9 KJV

We urge you, brethren, admonish the unruly,
encourage the fainthearted, help the weak,
be patient with everyone.

I Thessalonians 5:14 NASB